TRUE STORIES • HIDDEN FACTS

SHIPWRECKS

Anita Ganeri & David West

D1493540

WAYLAND
www.waylandbooks.co.uk

CONTENTS

INTRODUCTION

The ocean floor is littered with the wrecks of ships lost or destroyed at sea. Some ran aground on rocks or coral reefs; others ran into bad weather or sank in battle. Many have been rediscovered by divers using the latest in underwater technology. Their stories make fascinating reading, as they offer up their secrets from the deep.

 LIFT THE FLAP
TO FIND OUT MORE

SINKING OF THE MARY ROSE

'I'm afraid she's lost sire, lost!'

As the courtier whispered these words into the king's ear, a gasp went up from the crowd. Before their horrified eyes, the Mary Rose, the king's flagship, began to roll over and sink…

It was 19 July 1545. England was at war with France, and the Mary Rose was leading out the English fleet to fight the French in the English Channel. From nearby Plymouth, King Henry VIII watched with pride as the Mary Rose fired a broadside at the enemy ships, then swung round so that the guns on its other side could fire. Then disaster struck…

As the wind picked up, the ship tipped sharply to one side, and water rushed in through its open gun ports.

In an instant, in front of their very eyes, the once-proud Mary Rose rolled over and started to sink. The cries of the terrified crew carried across the water to the crowd. But there was little chance of escape…

LIFT THE FLAP
TO FIND OUT MORE

DISCOVERY OF THE TITANIC

'The sheer size of her is awesome!'

Through the portholes of their submersible, Alvin, Robert Ballard and his colleagues peered in amazement at the enormous, ghostly, grey shape. The sight sent shivers down their spines. Right in front of them rose the massive steel hull of RMS Titanic, the largest passenger liner of its day and a symbol of disaster for the 20th century. For Ballard, it was a dream come true. A year after first locating the wreck almost four kilometres down on the sea bed of the North Atlantic Ocean, he was now back for a closer look.

More surprises lay in store. On his second dive, Ballard could clearly see the rust-covered bow, with the huge anchors still in place. The following day, Alvin landed next to the Grand Staircase – a sombre reminder of the ship's grandeur. Using Jason Junior, a robotic camera, Ballard spotted a huge chandelier and peeked inside some of the first-class cabins. Exploring the Titanic was like wandering through a ghost town…

It had once been a very different story. Nicknamed 'the Millionaires' Special', the Titanic was built of the finest steel and fitted out in the grandest style, with a theatre, swimming pool, squash court and Turkish bath among its many attractions. On 14 April 1912, the ship was four days into its maiden voyage from Southampton to New York. Throughout the day, other ships in the area sent warnings of icebergs drifting further south than was usual for this time of year. On board the Titanic, the warnings were ignored.

Then, at 11.40pm, one of the look-outs spotted a gigantic iceberg dead ahead. Immediately, the order was given to swing the ship to one side but it was too late. The iceberg gashed a hole in Titanic's side and water began pouring in. A few minutes later, it came to a halt. Could it be that the ship labelled 'practically unsinkable' was sinking fast?

LIFT THE FLAP
TO FIND OUT MORE

HUNT FOR THE BISMARCK

'Stay on target! Torpedo away!'

With these words, the crew of the tiny Swordfish bomber launched another torpedo. Below, in the near darkness, lay its target – the German Navy's mighty Bismarck – the biggest warship afloat.

At dusk on 26 May 1941, the Swordfish, along with its squadron, scrambled from the aircraft-carrier, Ark Royal. Hampered by atrocious weather, this was to be its final attack. The crew watched nervously…as a huge column of smoke rose from the Bismarck's side. The torpedo – a shot in a million – had struck home! The ship began turning helplessly in a huge circle…the strike had disabled its steering gear.

Accompanied by the Prinz Eugen, the Bismarck's mission was to attack cargo ships in the North Atlantic Ocean ferrying supplies between the USA and Britain. Meanwhile, under orders to 'sink the Bismarck', the British Navy was determined to hunt the ship down. A fleet of warships and heavy cruisers, among them HMS Hood, flagship of the British fleet, had been dispatched. Then disaster struck. In an exchange of fire, the Hood had been directly hit by a shell from the Bismarck, exploded with a gigantic bang and sank. But the Bismarck was not safe yet.

Having already been badly hit, the ship was heading towards the safe water of a French harbour, when the Swordfish torpedo struck… Next day, the British fleet closed in and opened fire. Despite the pounding, the ship remained afloat for almost three hours, still flying its flag. Then, finally, at 10.38am on 27 May, the mighty Bismarck sank. Of the crew of 2,065, only 115 survived. But was that the end of the story?

LIFT THE FLAP
TO FIND OUT MORE

WRECK OF THE WHYDAH

'It's gold! Pirates' gold!'

The diver could not believe his eyes, as he gazed at the coin in his hand. And there was more to come. Soon, he and his fellow divers were unearthing not only thousands of gold and silver coins but pistols, anchors and other pieces of treasure…pirate treasure.

It was 1984. The divers were led by underwater explorer, Barry Clifford. Relying on an 18th-century map, Clifford had located the wreck of the Whydah, the flagship of infamous pirate, 'Black Sam' Bellamy. It had sunk in a storm off Cape Cod, USA, on 26 April 1717, taking most of its crew and treasure down with it.

Bellamy's pirate spree began in the Caribbean, raiding any ships that crossed his path. It took a three-day chase to capture the Whydah but it was worth the wait. The ship was sailing from Jamaica to England with a dazzling cargo of sugar, gold, silver and ivory. Realising resistance was useless, the captain surrendered…and escaped with his life.

Next, Bellamy headed northwards along the east coast of America, intent on continuing his trail of plunder. Then, on 26 April, disaster struck. As black clouds rolled in from the horizon, a fierce storm began to blow up. Sailing dangerously close to the coast, the Whydah was heading straight into it…

LIFT THE FLAP
TO FIND OUT MORE

ATTACK OF THE FIRESHIPS

'Flee, flee for your lives – the fireships are coming!'

As the horrified lookout shouted out his warning, he knew it was already too late. Staring out to sea, he could see that the tiny pinpricks of light were approaching the harbour…fast. With the wind blowing them towards the shore, the town's fate would soon be sealed. For the specks of light were burning ships, filled with hay or brushwood, then set on fire and sent to destroy the town of Hedeby…

It was just before dawn in the year 1050. The people of Hedeby, the most important trading centre in Viking Denmark, were just waking up. Hedeby was a busy place, its houses clustered closely together, along streets leading down to the sea. The town was protected on three sides by earthworks, leaving the harbour the only open approach. Its inhabitants had been feeling safe…until now.

As the look-out's warning rang out, all eyes turned towards the harbour where the fireships were bearing down. These were Norwegian ships, sent by King Harald Hardrada to score a victory over the Danish king. As the ships entered the harbour, they set light first to the other boats, then the flames spread to the town's wooden buildings. Hedeby was doomed. By the evening, the town had burned to the ground, despite desperate efforts to save it.

After Harald Hardrada's devastating attack, Hedeby was attacked and destroyed again in 1066. Its people abandoned their homes and moved across the water to the town of Schleswig. Hedeby lay forgotten and rising sea levels submerged it under the water. Then, almost 900 years later, divers made an exciting discovery…the remains of a Viking longship in the harbour. Could this have been one of Harald's fireships? All the signs pointed to it…

LIFT THE FLAP
TO FIND OUT MORE

LOSS OF THE MONITOR

'The boiler room's flooded - it's every man for himself!'

As he spoke, Captain John Bankhead knew his ship was doomed. For hours, the USS Monitor had been lashed by heavy seas and, at times, completely submerged. Now, the water had reached the boiler room and extinguished the fires that produced steam to power the engine and pumps. Despite the crew's valiant attempts to keep the water at bay, the Monitor was sinking…fast.

Under tow by the USS Rhode Island, the Monitor was approaching Cape Hatteras, and the area known as the 'Graveyard of the Atlantic'. It had been ordered north to Beaufort, North Carolina, from its base in Hampton Roads. The Monitor had already made history as the first ironclad warship in the US Navy. But, though well suited to river combat, its new and revolutionary design made the ship highly unstable in rough seas.

Realising that everything possible had been done to save the boat, Bankhead gave the order to abandon ship and get into the two approaching rescue boats. Several men remained behind, rooted to the spot with fear. Others were washed overboard by the waves. After unloading the men on to the Rhode Island, the boats returned to the Monitor, only to find they had arrived too late.

Just after midnight on 31 December 1862, the shell-shocked survivors aboard the Rhode Island watched in horror as the Monitor's lights went out and it sank beneath the sea. As day finally broke, nothing of this once-great ship was visible above the waves. Would the American people ever see the historic Monitor again?

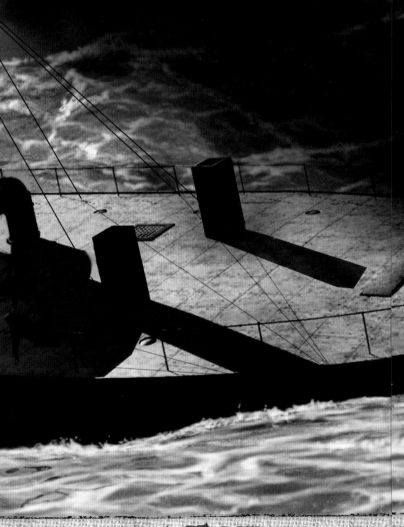

LIFT THE FLAP
TO FIND OUT MORE

DE LA SALLE'S LOST SHIP

'That's it - I believe this trip is truly cursed.'

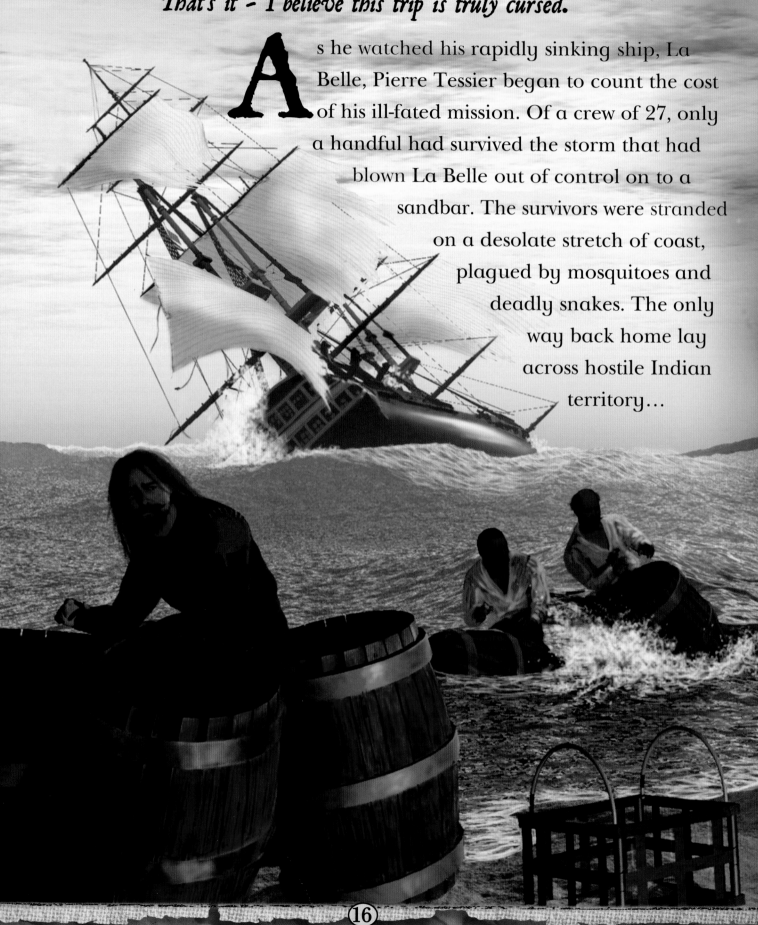

As he watched his rapidly sinking ship, La Belle, Pierre Tessier began to count the cost of his ill-fated mission. Of a crew of 27, only a handful had survived the storm that had blown La Belle out of control on to a sandbar. The survivors were stranded on a desolate stretch of coast, plagued by mosquitoes and deadly snakes. The only way back home lay across hostile Indian territory…

La Belle was one of four ships on an expedition to North America, led by French nobleman, Robert de La Salle. Having made his fortune in the fur trade, he now had the king's blessing to establish a French colony at the mouth of the Mississippi River. The ships reached the Gulf of Mexico in November 1684 but failed to find the delta. Instead, they landed at Matagorda Bay in Texas, 650 kilometres off course.

Having established a fort on the coast, de La Salle set off in La Belle to explore further afield, then left the ship in Tessier's command. With no sign of de La Salle, Tessier took the fateful decision to return to the fort. The storm that had blown La Belle aground left it just half a kilometre off the shore. For the next few days, the survivors salvaged as much as they could. But La Belle was already sinking and, for the next three centuries, the ship lay buried in murky waters on the bay…

LIFT THE FLAP
TO FIND OUT MORE

TREASURE OF THE ATOCHA

'It's no good, Captain, we can't get her hatches open!'

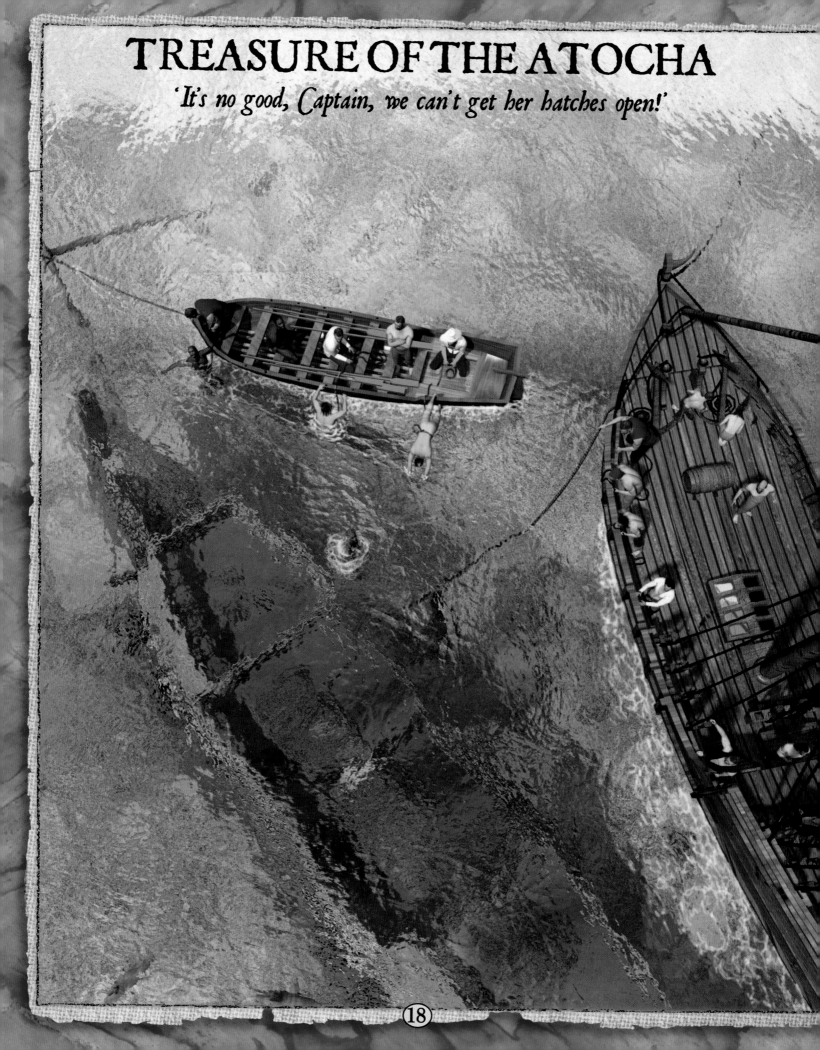

The diver, a local man, gasped for breath as he gave his report to the captain of the waiting boat. He was more used to diving for pearls in the waters around the Caribbean islands than searching for the booty from a treasure ship.

Like the rest of his team, his instructions had been simple – to dive down to the wreck of the Spanish galleon, and salvage as much of its treasure as possible. Along with six other ships, it had been caught up in a storm and wrecked a few days earlier off the Florida Keys, sinking under the weight of its valuable cargo. But the Spanish officials who had ordered the search were going to be disappointed – the hatches and portholes of the ship's cargo hold were locked. All they could rescue were two bronze cannon because another storm was on its way and the salvage boat was forced back to the harbour. The second storm scattered the remains of the ship, so that when the divers returned all signs of the wreckage were gone.

A few weeks earlier, Nuestra Señora de Atocha (Our Lady of Atocha), had loaded up with hundreds of gold and silver ingots, thousands of silver coins and large numbers of uncut emeralds at the Spanish ports of Cartagena in Colombia and Portobelo in Panama. The ship also carried valuable jewellery, tobacco, rosewood, indigo and copper.

After a series of delays, the fleet left Havana, Cuba, for Spain on 4 September 1622. It was six weeks behind schedule and sailing straight into the hurricane season.

Within two days, a violent storm drove the fleet on to the treacherous coral reefs off Florida Keys. With its hull badly damaged, the Atocha, and all its treasure, sank quickly. Only five of the Atocha's crew - three sailors and two slaves – were rescued. Despite the best efforts of the Spanish, the ship and its fabulous treasure seemed destined to lie forgotten on the bed of the sea…

LIFT THE FLAP
TO FIND OUT MORE

RMS LUSITANIA

'She's sinking fast. Let's down periscope and run for home.'

As Kapitanleutnant Schweiger spoke, he watched the stricken British liner list to starboard and begin to sink beneath the waves. His job here done, there was still the risk of his German U-20 submarine being rammed or fired on. It was time to head for home.

It was early afternoon on 7 May 1915. Britain and Germany had been at war for nine months. The liner, RMS Lusitania, was on its way from New York to Liverpool, with almost 3,000 passengers and crew on board.

Passengers had been warned that the Atlantic Ocean was now a war zone. That meant that any ship flying a British flag was in danger of being destroyed by German submarines. However none of those on board truly believed that Germany would carry out its threat and attack an unarmed passenger steamer.

On 7 May, the Lusitania was around 50 kilometres off the south coast of Ireland where she encountered fog and had to reduce her speed. With only a few hours to go until she reached her home port, she crossed right in front of the U-20…

The torpedo struck the Lusitania under its bridge, sending a plume of water, metal and debris into the air. Then a few minutes later, an even bigger explosion ripped the liner's starboard bow apart. The ship's captain sent out an SOS and gave the order to abandon ship. Immediately the ship began to list badly, giving the passengers little chance to escape. Just 18 minutes after being hit, the Lusitania sank beneath the waves.

Of the 1,959 people on board, some 1,198 were killed but a huge controversy over their deaths was only just beginning…

LIFT THE FLAP
TO FIND OUT MORE

ENIGMA OF THE U-110

'Now this is a prize even Blackbeard would have been proud of!'

As the Royal Navy destroyer HMS Bulldog drew alongside the wounded German submarine, Captain Baker-Cresswell knew that the prize he had been waiting for was finally within his grasp. It was 9 May 1941. Commanded by Kapitanleutnant Lemp, the U-110 had already been badly damaged in an earlier depth charge. As her crew scrambled desperately on to the decks, HMS Bulldog and Broadway were waiting to open fire…

But instead of using their deck gun, the crew of the U-110 had been given the order to abandon ship. Seeing the German sailors trying to leave the ship, the British gave the order to cease fire. Bulldog and Broadway closed in to capture the U-boat and stop it from sinking. Like his crew, Lemp, too, believed the boat was sinking and abandoned ship. When he realised she was still afloat, he desperately tried to swim back again to make sure the British didn't get hold of the U-110's secret cargo…

Lemp did not make it back to the U-110 and would never be seen again. Instead, the Bulldog's crew boarded the boat and stripped it of everything they could carry. Among the items they found was the cargo that Lemp was so desperate to keep from them – top secret German codebooks and an Enigma machine. But the sailors had to be very careful. The codebooks had been printed in ink that would dissolve if the books were dropped in sea water.

Anxious to ensure that the Germans knew nothing about the U-110's capture, and so did not change their codes, it was nicknamed 'Operation Primrose' and every sailor was sworn to secrecy. It would remain one of the biggest secrets of World War II. Meanwhile, the U-110 itself was towed back to Britain and 'accidentally' sank on the way home. For the time being, her secret was going to be safe…

LIFT THE FLAP
TO FIND OUT MORE

GLOSSARY

Archaeologist A person who studies the past by looking at ancient places and objects. Marine archaeologists study underwater places.

Artefact A man-made object of archaeological interest from the past.

Cofferdam A watertight structure that surrounds an area underwater that is pumped dry so work can be carried out.

Earthworks Man-made banks of earth. They used to be built as fortifications to protect a town, such as those around Hedeby.

Flagship The most important ship in a fleet. The ship belonging to the commander of the fleet.

Galley A type of ship propelled by sails or oars that was used in ancient and medieval times.

Ironclad A 19th century warship made from iron or wood and protected by iron armour plating.

Salvage To save or rescue goods from a ship wrecked at sea.

Submersible A small craft that is designed to explore underwater.

Telemotor The control system for the Titanic's steering gear.

INDEX